Prayers for Crown Jewels

In her beautiful testament *Prayers for Crown Jewels*, Karen so candidly presents the heartbreaking oppression, poverty, and spiritual battles afflicting the world's women and children. Yet there is hope! Our Jesus has the power to transform hearts, lives, and nations, and these powerful prayers offer an effective blueprint for world-changing intercession.

—John C. Boyd, President and CEO, Mission Aviation Fellowship

Do you sense an urgency to pray for women in war-torn lands but feel overwhelmed by cultural differences, not knowing how to pray for those with needs vastly different than yours? Karen Carlson leads the reader through powerful model prayers that uniquely petition the Lord for the harassed and destitute woman. Using the names of God revealed throughout Scripture, Karen reminds us how Jesus Christ cherishes women, who are undervalued and too often seen as worthless, as Crown Jewels. This is a wonderful resource for anyone wanting to be obedient to pray with impact for those she may never meet until heaven.

—Shawn Lantz, speaker and author of *Encountering the Healing Power of Forgiveness* and *Living With Unmet Desires: Exposing the Many Faces of Jealousy*

We live in a world where countless women and children, preciously created in God's image, endure abuse, slavery, trafficking, hunger, violence and so much more. The need seems overwhelming, the war unwinnable. But in *Prayers for Crown Jewels*, author Karen Carlson reminds us that prayer is not the least of weapons. The book's thirty-day format with prayers, challenges, and resources helps any reader--or prayer warrior--become intentional in waging this war through prayer on behalf of women and children at risk worldwide. May each of us accept the challenge!

—Jeanette Windle, author of *Veiled Freedom, Freedom's Stand,* and *Congo Dawn*

Having lived and worked for more than 40 years in some of the poorest and most war torn parts of the world, I rejoice to see this book come into being. Together we can make a difference through our prayers. Recently I have been involved in a trauma healing ministry to deeply hurting, wounded people. It means so much to them to hear that God's people around the world are remembering and praying for them. Don't let this book sit on a shelf. Use it every day and wear it out! One day in heaven you will meet thousands of people who were rescued from unspeakable horror in answer to your faithful prayers!

—Cami Robbins, Wycliffe Bible Translators, USA

PRAYERS FOR CROWN JEWELS

Honoring Women and Children in a World at War

Karen Deits Carlson

Mobikisi Press Eaton Colorado

Prayers for Crown Jewels
Honoring Women and Children in a World at War

All proceeds from the sale of this book go toward ministries that work with at-risk women and children. See www.prayersforcrown-jewels.com for more details.

Prayers are based on scriptures taken from the NEW AMERICAN STANDARD BIBLE®, COPYRIGHT © 1960, 1962, 1963, 1968, 1971, 1972, 1973, 1975, 1977, 1995 by The Lockman Foundation. Used by permission. www.Lockman.org.

The publisher does not have any control over and does not assume any responsibility for third-party websites or their content.

ISBN: 978-0-9914568-0-2

Dedicated to the Only One

Who can set the captives free

The LORD their God will save His people on that day

as a shepherd saves his flock.

They will sparkle in his land

like *jewels in a crown.*

Zechariah 9:16 (NIV)

Contents

Notes for further reflection and prayer

Preface

The conflict began with Eve. Satan knew her God-given nature was more trusting, more nurturing, and less aggressive than Adam's. It was no mistake that he singled her out. He would do whatever it took to mar the image of the One he hated, the One who had all the best of femininity as well as masculinity. His tactics haven't changed over the millennia.

Half of humanity is female. If that half is not honored and appreciated with purpose and dignity as created equally before God, then abuse, perversion, and hatred of women follows. Oppression and poverty trail after, affecting all in society: men, women, children, and the unborn. No period in history, including our own, is exempt from the horrors inflicted upon women and children. The current facts and figures of individuals made in the image of God within this prayer battle plan are staggering—defined in terms of millions and billions. We can close our eyes and ears to what is happening today. But with the advent of globalization, we will find it in our own backyard soon. Some already have.

These women and children have been tagged as "disposable", "forgotten", "hidden". Many ministries and organizations are working tirelessly to ease their burden. They are making a difference; but it is not enough. The challenges are colossal. Different beliefs, cultures, governments, and problematic threads interweave in the carpet in this war against women and children. Because these *crown jewels* live "under the radar", just about anything can be done to them...and it is. Slavery. Domestic violence. Genital mutilation. Trafficking. Bride burning. Acid throwing. Rape. Sexual abuse. Oppression. Poverty. Abortion. Malnutrition. AIDS. Infant mortality...

One day we will stand before a holy God to give an account of how we spent the time He gave us here on earth. Will we take up in the power of the Spirit the armor He has given us to fight against the rulers, powers, and world and spiritual forces of this wicked darkness? Many of the victims caught in these dark webs do not even know the name of Jesus. What a responsibility and privilege we have to pray for them!

Jesus said He was the Light of the World. He commanded us to walk as children of the Light and not hide under a basket. Our prayers for the least of these are a fragrant offering unto Him.

One candle, one prayer,
in the darkness can give light.
Thousands can drive the
darkness away.

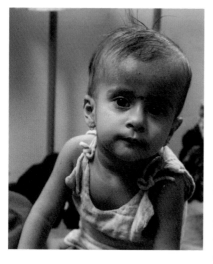

There are over 30 million in our world today who are suffering slavery, sexual abuse, and/or oppression. Many, if not most, of us are unaware of these issues facing primarily women and children. Once made aware, we want to help, to be a part of the solution. But we don't know how. We also are not sure that it would make a difference. God has given us families and jobs and ministries right where we are. How can we drop everything to go stand alongside those who are hurting? If there was only a way...

There is a way. We can confidently approach the very throne of God and stand as an advocate for these distressed women and children. Jesus said if we do anything for the least of our brethren, we do it unto Him. These are precious souls who are hidden away from the public eye. They feel forgotten, abandoned, and hopeless. God is the only One who knows exactly what each one needs today; He is the only One who can give help that will last. It is to our loving heavenly Father that we must go.

This book contains a prayer strategy for thirty prayers covering a wide range of topics that affect oppressed and broken women and children in today's world of globalization. In theory, one focus for each day of the month. But let's face it. Life or our children or our work or our husband/wife or an illness has an uncanny and surprising way of interfering and interrupting our best intentions. I'm a wife of a missionary pilot living in a third-world country with seven children to boot. Most of the past twenty-eight years on the field have had unexpected turns and challenges. You have your own, probably different from mine.

So in practice, I use a paper clip or bookmark to keep track of where I am. Some days I can get to three prayers; some weeks I only pray through two. My hope is that by the end of the month I am caught up. Honestly, I rarely am. But sometime during the year I usually am. That is what counts. I'm being consistent, in my own unique way, on praying through matters that count for eternity, that are life and death for someone. Here's encouragement for a parent with little ones in the house, or an individual just setting up a new business, or ___ (you fill in the blank). We don't have to give up just because we "got off the schedule". We keep praying for the prayer before us, and on the days we have a little more time, we work through two or three.

I have two copies. One stays in a heavy-duty plastic zippered bag. It can go with me on the road, while standing in line, and while sitting in an office. What a great way to redeem those minutes that vanish before me waiting for something or someone! You can bring yours to your Bible study and pray together while waiting for the others to arrive. Perhaps when you read or hear about an issue facing women or children and you don't know what to pray biblically, turn to the corresponding page to give you an idea of what to pray. Use these prayers and scriptures in whatever way works *for you*.

Each prayer is only a suggestion. Think of it as a place to start. Learn to be quiet before the Lord to listen to more of what He wants you to pray. In the back of the book are current facts and figures for contemplation and to provide a few resources should God be leading you to do more research. By no means is it comprehensive.

Prayer is not glamorous or enticing. It *can* sometimes be spectacular and sensational. However, many of our answers we won't see until heaven. What joy awaits us to hear Jesus' words of, "Well done, thou good and faithful servant!" And then He will step aside to show us the thousands (dare we believe God for millions!) of women and children whose lives or circumstances were changed because we prayed. Keep at it, follower of Christ, in the power of the Spirit. Be fervent. Be faithful. The women and children of our world are desperate for release.

To comfort all who mourn,

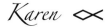

1. Access to Scripture

Dear heavenly Father, hundreds of millions in our world do not have even a portion of Your Word in their heart language. They cannot believe and call upon You if they do not know what You have said. Raise up more men and women who are willing to study many years to gain the skills necessary for Bible translation work. Provide the finances they need to acquire the training without going into great debt so they are able to quickly begin working in the fields ripe for harvest.

Strengthen those who are laboring long hours translating the Bible into their target language. Give them cultural keys that will open accurately Your truth to the people group for which they toil. Many are struggling with difficult and hostile situations. Provide for their spiritual, mental, emotional, financial, physical, and family needs. Bring more native speakers who have a heart for and the ability to express Your Word in their own language.

Your people are destroyed for lack of knowledge. May women and children around the world come to know and keep Your statutes. Any man, woman, or child is blessed who meditates on Your Word. As each delights in Your laws, You reveal more and more of Yourself to them as well as bless, strengthen, protect, revive, and comfort them. How great and awesome are You, the God of heaven! Your Word will endure forever.

Encourage today those women and children who find themselves in situations where it would be impossible to believe Your promises apart from Your Holy Spirit's work in their lives. You can sympathize with and understand their struggles for even Your Son was beaten beyond recognition, abandoned, and forgotten at the cross. Yet through it all, He clung to Scripture.

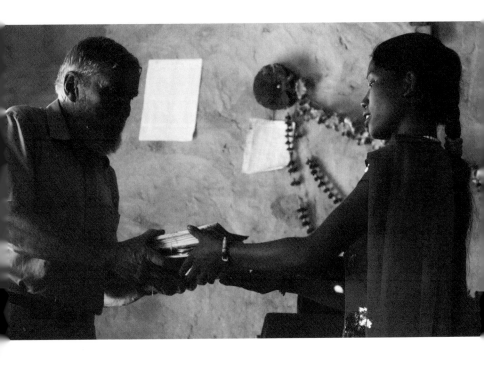

Jn. 4:35; Hos. 4:6; Ps. 1:2; Ps. 119;
Neh. 1:5; Heb. 4:14, 15

2. Blessing of the Land & Farming

All of creation groans, waiting eagerly for the time when the effects of weeds, thorns, pestilence, drought, and famine will be broken, and the earth will be as it was in the beginning before sin entered the world. So much has gone wrong in our fulfilling the role You gave us in Eden to care for and protect creation.

May the women in each nation who are followers of Christ repent of any innocent bloodshed, wrongs, idolatries, and abominations. Even more will humble themselves, pray, and seek Your face. Then as each woman prays in the power of the Holy Spirit over the land You have provided, she will experience Your blessing and Your bounty. Bring people and resources into her life to show her how to increase the fertility and usefulness of the land and water. In faith she will come out and shout for joy for Your supernatural provision. Her neighbors will stand in awe of You, *Jehovah-Jireh* (the LORD our Provider).

Bless the work of those who eke out a meager, subsistent existence. Because of the atoning work of Christ, You are able and willing to make up for the years that the locusts have eaten so there will be plenty to eat. All will see Your merciful hand and praise Your name. Only You can change dry, unfruitful ground into a land flowing with milk and honey. Open the heavens and bring the right amount of rain in its season. The produce of the ground will abound in Your prosperity. You will bless their baskets and their kneading bowls.

For those in war-torn areas where it is difficult or dangerous to work, bring peace and safety. We ask for guardian angels to surround and protect women and children as they travel to and from their gardens.

Hos. 4:2-3; Rom. 8:19-22; 2 Chr. 7:14; Jer. 31:12;
Gen. 22:13-14; Joel 2:25-26; Deut. 28: 4-12

3. Businesses by Women

El-Olam (Everlasting God), may businesswomen have a tender heart for other women and children, especially widows in their midst. May they never be tempted to use cheap slave labor or compromise Your holy standard. Use these business leaders to stir up and expose the dark side of business. Give them the integrity and determination to work righteousness and refuse to walk alongside companies who oppress and abuse women and children. This might mean temporary setbacks in terms of finances, influence, and progress. However, the godly women, who walk in Your ways in their businesses, will ultimately and for eternity be blessed. Your Son, the Cornerstone, will be the foundation and focus of their businesses.

Especially bless women with micro-businesses around the world who are struggling to provide the basic necessities for their families. Bring others into their lives who can teach them sound business protocol and ethical probity. Increase the ministries of those organizations and people who are striving to aid poverty-stricken women with micro financing. May we, Your children, freely open our hand to the needy and poor around the world so they will have access to needed finances. You empowering these women will strengthen societies and economies around the world.

The governments and societal norms around them can easily oppress many women legally. Bring true legal help to those who are experiencing barriers in their place of work. Shield them from all forms of sexual harassment and assault. Supernaturally grow businesses and individuals who will create safe work places. May women in the work force be paid fair and comparable wages. Transform the hearts of those men throughout the world who do not want women to grow and develop the gifts and abilities You have given them.

Is. 40:28-31; Ps. 15:2; Prov. 4:14; 2 Pet. 1:2-11; Deut. 15:11

4. Church Leaders Become Shepherds

King David proclaimed You as *Jehovah-Rohi* (the LORD is my Shepherd). Furthermore, Father, You sent Jesus to be the Shepherd of our Souls. He was the perfect example of how to care for His flock. Even though He was the Son of God, He did not demand special attention or preferential treatment. The needs of His flock were ever present in His mind. He was never too busy. He valued women far more than the culture of the day dictated. Little children were always welcomed into His arms. Jesus loved and attended to the lost, the broken, and the needy — regardless of their gender or their age.

Today many whom You have called to be a shepherd have themselves lost their way. They destroy and scatter Your sheep. Woe to those who look out merely for their own personal interest and not those of Jesus. Pour out Your Spirit upon these church leaders around the world. Then they will be known for their love, compassion, and watchful care of the flock that You have given them. By the power of Your Spirit, they will not lead your children off Your path but straight to You, their only Resting Place. Stir up their spirits to follow Your leading. They will find a perfect mentor in You.

You hate pride, haughtiness, sexual sin, and arrogance in Your people, especially in church leaders. Teach them to serve rather than to be served. Let men in leadership be role models in regard to loving and serving their wives as Your Son serves the church.

Only through the power of Your Spirit are they able to set the example to strengthen the sick, heal the diseased, bind up the broken, bring back the scattered, and seek the lost.

Ps. 23:1; I Pet. 2:25; Mic. 5:1-5; Jer. 50:6; Jer. 23:1;
Phil. 2:21; Hag. 1:14; Ez. 34:3-4

5. Church/Missionary Access

Jesus is eternal Life, the Truth, and the only Way. There is no other name with the authority to save us. Anyone who has the Son of God has life. But millions around the world do not know even who the Redeemer is. Other millions have not understood the clear Gospel message of Jesus' sacrifice for their sins. How can these millions believe unless they hear? And how will they hear unless Your children go to them?

Open countries which have closed their borders to missionaries, Father. Empower nationals who know You to proclaim Your name and works. Grant a free access to each people group in our world. Through Your Holy Spirit, open their spirits and enlighten their eyes to Your great love and eternal plan for their lives. You have placed eternity in every heart. We wait with eagerness and faith for the culmination of history; where from each tribe and tongue and nation, those washed in Your Son's blood will worship You with a new song.

These missionary ambassadors will increase in Your grace so that they might willing work at what brings You pleasure. Their ever-increasing love for You and for others will gain them friends and influence in key positions. Grow them in the works and ministry of the Holy Spirit, especially in countries that historically have had hard ground.

As these sent-ones pray according to Your will, *Elohim* (God), answer them with amplified provision and ministry opportunities. Open their eyes to where the field is white for harvest in the areas where they serve. Equip them with increased boldness to preach the Gospel to the dying. They will not labor in vain as You build Your house upon the Rock, Your Son. May millions turn to You with believing faith.

Jn. 14:6; Acts 4:12; Rom. 10:14,15; Rev. 5:9; Phil. 2:13;
Matt. 22:37-40; Jn. 4:35; Ps. 127:1

6. Corruption, Lying, & Stealing

Dear Father, You have clearly told us what is good for mankind. You require us to do justice, to love kindness, and to walk humbly with You. When we fail, You see it all, *El-Roi* (the Strong One Who Sees).

We have confidence to enter boldly into the Holy Place because of the blood of Jesus. Therefore, we take a stand against the corruption, lying, and stealing in this world and in Your church. It is not Your way or Your plan. Break the bonds that enslave these leaders to corruption, and may they find freedom in Jesus. In the power of Your Spirit, they will not walk in the counsel of the wicked or be overcome by the intense pressure of those around them who desire to do what is wrong. In You, men and women in positions of authority are granted everything they need to live in godliness. So many leaders stumble in living with integrity because of living under the lure of power or the love of money. Where, O God, are the men and women who are willing to walk in Your ways and appear as lights in the world? Increase their numbers.

Smash the corruption of organized crime and of bribes to police, border patrols, and judges which shatters millions of women and children. Let their days be few and others take their offices. Deliver those women and children who have been or are being robbed. May their oppressors fall. Destroy those who speak falsely. Install more men and women who will not be partial, who cannot be bought to look the other way, or who will not actively aid those who do evil.

You, Faithful God, keep Your covenant and loving kindness to those who love You and obey Your laws.

Jer. 22:3; Heb. 10:19; 2 Pet. 2:19-20; Ps. 1:1; 2 Pet. 1:3;
Deut. 16:19; Ps. 109:7-8; Ps. 5:6

7. Discipleship & Spiritual Growth

Adonai (Lord of my life), Your Son is the True Vine; we are the branches. In order to bear more spiritual fruit, You prune each branch. It is not typically enjoyable. Some women and children are going through intense pruning right now. Encourage each one today to know that their circumstances are not more than they can bear, although humanly, it looks like they are.

As Corrie ten Boom said, "There is no pit so deep that God is not deeper still." Grow these suffering ones so their roots stretch down to find the sweet Living Water. You will work far more abundantly in their lives than what they can even dream about. Some women and children have been so traumatized by people in the church that they want nothing to do with You. Break down the walls and replant their Faith Garden.

You call every believer, no matter what nationality or what circumstance, to be a follower of You, Jesus. Doing Your Father's will was all that mattered. It is all that matters today as well. That great and fraudulent master, money, will not have claim over these women and children's lives. Instead, they will ask for and receive wisdom from above so they can be imitators of You.

We are to reflect You in all that we do so that the world will see our good works and give You the glory You deserve. Women and children all over the world have that opportunity to shine Your light in the darkest holes. You will not fail them. Your physically-broken, but spiritually-alive children will shout along with the apostle Paul, "For me to live is Christ and to die is gain!" Many will be encouraged as they see the spiritual depth in these lives. Your name will be magnified forever!

Jn. 15:1-2; Eph. 3:20; Jam. 1:5; Eph. 5:1; Matt. 5:16;
Phil. 1:21; 2 Sam. 7:26

8. Education of Girls & Freedom from Sexual Harassment

Heavenly Father, You place a high priority on reading and meditating on Your Word. You bless those individuals who read and hear Your words. Throughout history, disastrous errors came into Your Church and cultures when the general populous became illiterate. When the few and powerful are the only individuals who know how to read, personal liberties are minimal or non-existent.

The more education a girl has, the less likely she is to be a victim of prostitution, slavery, poverty, and violence. Stir up the hearts of girls and women around the world to hunger for truth and wisdom in all areas of life. Break down the barriers of gender preference for the financing for schooling and education. Supernaturally provide funding for those families who do not have the means to send all their children to school, especially difficult when the girls reach secondary school. Soften the hearts of fathers who believe that education will only ruin or compromise their wives and daughters. Bless these girls with Your wisdom as well as the commitment to finish secondary school.

When girls do attend school, protect them from sexual harassment or harm from male teachers, school leaders, and/or other students. Provide safe environments where girls and women can learn. Bring down the high illiteracy rate of women around the world. Open up innovative venues where young women can learn skills and trades so they can help supplement their families' incomes. Spark creative ideas for new home businesses especially where women and girls do not yet have much freedom outside the home.

We desire that whatever teaching is done follows Your guidelines: those things which are true, honorable, right, pure, lovely, of good repute, excellent, and worthy of praise. May Your Word be the strong foundation of all they are taught and learn.

Rev. 1:3; Ps. 25:4-5; Phil. 4:8

9. An End to the Wicked

Father, You are slow to anger. You do not feel any pleasure in the death of the wicked. Your desire is for them to turn, to repent, to be restored, and to walk in Your ways. You offer forgiveness to each and every one of those guilty of not keeping Your holy standard even to the one who has been responsible for despicable acts against women and children. That is Your Father-heart.

However, Your righteousness cannot tolerate the wicked in Your presence, O Consuming Fire. It is terrifying to fall into Your hands, O Living God. Convict the wicked. May they truly rend their hearts before You and not mock You or merely put on a show of penitence. We believe that evil men and women shall have a change of heart and thus put away violence and destruction. They will concentrate instead on practicing justice and righteousness.

The ungodly, who rejoice over the fall or death of the righteous, do not know that You are the salvation and light of the upright. We stand here and now in faith waiting expectantly for You, Lord God, to break through and deliver. In faith the praises of those who oppress the lowly will fall upon infertile ground. Confuse the counsel of those who rely on ungodly and unprincipled men and women. We proclaim that the unrepentant themselves will fall into the pits they dug for others!

Enough of those who expropriate the property of the poor for their own gain! You, Almighty, will by no means let the wicked go unpunished. You are jealous, avenging, and wrathful on those who continue in their wicked ways. Repay them according to their dealings. You maintain our just prayer. How majestic is Your name!

Nah 1:2-3; Ez. 18:23; Deut. 4:24; Heb. 10:31; Mic. 7:7-8;
Ps. 57:6; Ez. 45:9; Ps. 28:3-4

10. Equality of Women & Value as Individuals

Jehovah-Nissi (the LORD our Banner), there is no one who comes to You more worthy than another. We are all in need of Your grace and Your offer of redemption—whether we are Hindu, Muslim, Jew, Catholic, Protestant, Evangelical, Charismatic, or atheist; slave or free; female or male. Break down the dividing walls so all who are in Your Church see the unity of each disciple of Jesus equally bound together on the cross.

Open the eyes of Your children to see that all believers—men, women, and children alike—have every spiritual blessing in the heavenlies in Christ. We have equal access. We are joint-heirs. May this spiritual reality of equality for women become an earthly reality in matters of guardianship of their children, legal possession of their homes, lands, and goods, especially if their husbands die.

Mighty God, raise up more courageous men and women who are willing to fight for equality of women under the law. In faith these women dwell securely in the land and houses you have provided them. Execute judgment on those who want to grab it for themselves or scorn Your given-rights to women. Your Word teaches us to care for widows. Where there are cultural practices that adversely affect widows, raise up people who are willing to execute justice.

In matters of marriage, so many young women and girls are pawns forced into marriages by their families and society for power, prestige, and/or money. Unrealistic bride prices or dowries are used as a means to gain wealth. Bring changes in these cultures so each daughter is cherished as a jewel, precious in Your sight because of who they are and not because of how they can be used. Girls worldwide will learn to walk in that profound truth with purpose and dignity.

Ex. 17:15; Gal. 3:28; Eph. 1:3; Rom. 8:17; Ez. 34:27

11. Establish the Righteous in Key Positions

How blessed are those who do not associate in close fellowship and friendship with the ungodly. *Jehovah-Tsidkenu* (the LORD our Righteousness), purge those whose hearts are not on upholding Your righteousness but are bent on evil. Remove them from leadership positions until You find none. Establish more like Joseph—a man who forgave those who harmed him, who saw Your hand in all of his life, who worked diligently at what was given to him, who refused to be drawn away from Your holy standard, and who continued to seek after You. Most importantly, position men and women of integrity as leaders in Your church.

Raise up and train an army of men and women in each nation of the world who will labor passionately and steadfastly so that all under their rule, whether it be men, women, children, or the not-yet-born, will be able to lead a "tranquil and quiet life in all godliness and dignity." Gird them so they are willing to do what is right, even if it pains them.

Men of bloodshed hate the blameless. Protect and hide the righteous and their loved ones in the blood of Jesus so that they will suffer no retaliation or harm. Put a protective hedge of thorns around these servants; build a wall of defense so those who seek to do harm cannot penetrate the stronghold You have placed around the righteous. Instruct them in Your ways. Open their eyes to see You and their ears to hear Your voice.

Surround the upright with an abundance of godly counselors. But may they rest firmly and confidently in You, Wonderful Counselor, above all. As You give insight to those who seek You, may they shine Your righteousness and Your holiness like stars into their spheres of influence.

Ps. 1:1; I Kings 3:6; 1 Tim. 2:2; Jn. 3:20; Prov. 11:14; Is. 9:6; Matt. 5:16

12. Evangelism of the Lost

The whole world lies in the power of the evil one. The adversary roams to and fro in his domain seeking multitudes to devour. You sent Your Son, the Light of the World, to show us the way and to light our path back to You. Your desire is for all, women and children included, to be saved and to come to the knowledge of the truth. You are God, there is no other. Salvation comes only in the name of Jesus Christ the Nazarene. Nothing we do can save these precious lives for eternity, only You can save. Any who believe in Christ receive forgiveness of their sins.

The vast majority of women and children at-risk in this war do not know You as **Yahweh** (I AM). We praise You for Your faithfulness to search for and seek out any who have a hunger for more of You. You have promised to save all who call upon the name of Jesus. You are faithful to Your Word, for You do not want any to perish. You have promised to bring into Your family those from every tribe and tongue and people and nation.

Give Your soul winners fresh and relevant ways to proclaim that Jesus is the Way, the Truth, and the Life. Bless them with boldness and strength as they battle for the souls of the perishing.

In faith we, who already know the path of salvation, hold fast without wavering to support, aid, and encourage those who are sent to proclaim the Good News of Jesus Christ. These men and women need our finances, our prayers, our friendship, and our assistance. May we also daily look for opportunities to share the Gospel with those around us.

I Jn. 5:19; I Pet. 5:8; I Tim. 2:4; Is. 45:22; Acts 10:43;
Ez. 34:11; 2 Pet. 3:9; Rev. 5:9

13. The Family

Satan prowls about like a roaring lion seeking to destroy and devour Your most basic foundation for society, the family. In the power of Your Spirit, gird up those who call You by name to be on the alert and to resist the enemy. Restore and revive Christian marriages to be a reflection of every blessing You intended it to be. Consecrate men who love their wives and women who honor their husbands to be role models and mentors. Money woes, problem children, addictions, and infidelity can threaten even the strongest union if both the husband and wife are not centered in Christ.

Because You hate divorce, remind family members, especially husbands and wives, of the imperativeness to forgive, for the little things as well as the big. Your Spirit provides the means to forgive when others have harmed or wounded us. Continue to raise up godly fathers and mothers who understand and obey the important mandate to bring up and instruct their children in the knowledge and fear of You.

Millions of girls and women yearn for healing from what fathers, brothers, and/or other men in their families have done to them. In the very place where You designed protection—the family—these women and girls have found betrayal and evil. How Your Father-heart weeps! Because their own fathers or father figures have defrauded them, these women who need Your love and gift of salvation run from it. Remove the warped lens from their eyes so they can see and know You as their Loving Father. There is no other place where these priceless but blemished ones can come for healing. Only the blood of Christ can wash away the sin done to them. Only the blood of Christ can make these unfinished gems sparkle clean, pure, and bright.

Eph. 5:22-27; Mal. 2:16; Eph. 4:32; Prov. 1:7-8; Prov. 2:1-5

14. Forgiveness of Past Abuse/Wrongs

Millions of women and children today need You, O Comforter, as they struggle to make it through the day. Unbelievable horrors have been levied against them, who are made in Your likeness, who are reflections of Your glory. Wrong after wrong, year after year, they have hung on by a thread. Multitudes do not know that You are the Balm of Gilead, the only One who can soothe, heal, and restore.

Jesus taught to forgive those who harm and shatter everything near and dear. Remind them how much You have forgiven them. You know the abuse each one has faced and/or is facing today. May Your Holy Spirit bring to mind any unconfessed sin or person to forgive. In faith these women and children will resist the roots of bitterness, rage, and hopelessness to be planted in their spirits. You stand ready to gather these precious souls into Your arms enabling them to forgive their enemies or their families for their part in this abuse.

Because of the enemy's lies, some may even blame You. Many women have regrets over choices they made. Encourage them to forgive themselves. As each one reaches out in the power of the Holy Spirit to forgive, may You overwhelm them with peace and joy in their spirits. Only You can make that exchange. Use this in their lives to show others around them the difference of Christianity, which is Christ in them.

We acknowledge that Your loving-kindnesses and Your compassions never cease or fail. They are new every morning. Even though many circumstances cloud that truth, we believe that Your faithfulness is great. It is hard to understand that these women and children are blessed because You will embrace them in a way most of us will never experience.

Jer. 46:11; Matt. 18:21-22; Heb. 12:15; Matt. 5:44;
Jn. 14:26; Gal. 2:20; Lam. 3:22-23

15. Health Care & AIDS

Your desire is for us to come to You and to pray when any are suffering, *Jehovah-Rapha* (the LORD that Heals). Open Your ears to the cries from ill and disease-ridden women and children. Bless the many hospital and public health clinics around the world working under difficult and demanding situations. Raise up more skilled medical personnel to support Your work in medical missions. Open our hearts to give money and resources to buy needed equipment, supplies, and medicine.

Work in each government around the world to advance medical work in their country. What You are doing with the little that these hospitals and centers have is nothing short of miraculous! Praise Your name! Tropical and insect-borne diseases, sanitation and hygiene issues, and contaminated water are rampant in the developing world. Guide those who are researching cures and solutions to health problems. Open their eyes to see new ways of treating diseases.

Place efficient, trained men and women of integrity in administrative positions. They need Your balance of compassion and equity as they juggle overwhelming needs with limited resources. Gift them with creative responses. Empower them to run a tight ship for temptations to pilfer abound.

As women and children heal physically, bring alongside medical staff, chaplains, and pastors who can point the Way to emotional and spiritual healing. We cannot simply treat the body without attending to the soul and spirit.

Millions of women and children have health issues related to moral choices, either their own or someone else's. Forgive our judging those who have preventable diseases, especially STDs and AIDS. You alone, Holy Father, are Judge. Even Your Son Jesus did not come to judge the world, but to save those who are in darkness. Let us therefore pray for Your mercy and Your saving grace.

Jam. 5:13; Ex. 15:26; Mk. 2:3-12; Matt. 7:1; Jn. 12:47

16. Infant Mortality & Abortion

Diseases, which most children in the developed world can fight off, become life threatening in the developing world. In some areas, Father, infants are not even given a name for months, even years. Save the children of the needy, O God.

Your Son, the Living Water, understands the benefits of clean, life-saving water. Thousands of communities need outside aid to bring safe water to them. In addition, Your little ones need adequate housing, sanitation, food, and medical care so they can grow and fulfill the destiny You have for them. Show Your compassion to these wee ones. Bless their parents with adequate jobs so they can properly provide for the children You have given them. Bring more men and women alongside to teach and model simple but important well-being lifestyles. Give them fresh, creative, and sustainable ideas for healthier communities around the world.

Children are a gift from You. However, millions of babies, created by You and in Your image, are regarded as merely tissue in their mothers' wombs and are deemed as unwanted, inconvenient, or unworthy to live. Therefore these precious ones are aborted and thrown away. And if they are baby girls in many parts of the world, they are in greater risk. We grieve alongside You. In Your great mercy, Author of Life, save them. They did not have the chance to live out Your purpose for their lives. Bring to justice those who have aided in this carnage: health providers, government officials, or family and friends.

Heal emotionally those women, whether young or old, who have repented of abortions in the past and enable them to forgive themselves. Raise up an army of believers who are willing to give of their finances, their time, and their energy to fight in the battle for little children.

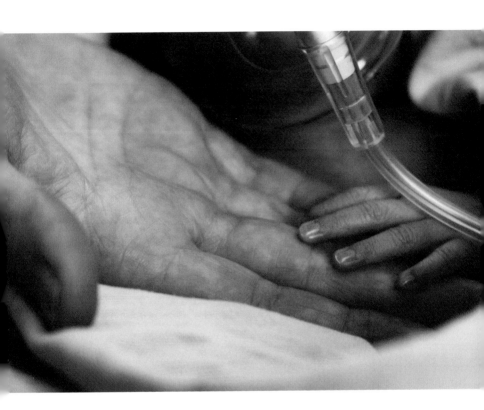

Ps. 72:4; Ps. 103:13; Ps. 127:3; Ps. 139:13-16;
Acts 3:15; Acts 20:35

17. Justice

To govern well, an individual must hate evil, wrong, and injustice. Teach Your servants of justice to fear You, *El-Elyon* (the Most High God). In faith, they will seek You daily and will delight in knowing Your ways. Then they will have the courage to be Your ministers to avenge those who practice evil. They themselves will walk in honesty and integrity.

Increase the numbers of men and women who are willing to pay the cost to bring justice according to Your Word. Blessed and Holy Ruler, grant them an anointing of Your Holy Spirit like You bestowed upon Solomon. Give them a discerning heart between good and evil, right and wrong. Open their ears to hear Your voice instructing them. May each defend the weak, the poor, the widows, and the fatherless. We need judges, lawyers, and law enforcement officers who will not look the other way because of age, color, gender, and/or ethnicity. May they not develop hearts of stone as they seek to serve their nation and community in difficult situations.

Correct, O Lawgiver, those who do not preserve justice, truth, and righteousness especially as it concerns women and children. If these government servants of Yours do not listen and obey Your correction, remove them from office. They will not primarily look out for their own personal interests.

We yearn for the day when all wrongs will be righted, all evil recompensed, and all injustice revealed. Until then, You have placed leaders in authority in each and every nation to execute righteousness, judgment, and justice and to uphold Your laws. Use them to execute justice for the oppressed. May they tread upon the lion and cobra in Your strength. Thank You for Jesus, Our Advocate, sitting on Your right hand speaking up for us.

Prov. 8:13; Is. 58:2; Rom.13:4; I Kings 3:9; Ps. 82:3-4;
Rom. 13:1; 2 Sam. 8:15; Ps. 91:13

18. Leaders & Fathers as Servants

The greatest example of servanthood is found in Your Son. Jesus spoke and the world was made. Since that time He has held all things together. Yet He did not insist on His rights as God but set aside those privileges to become a servant obediently following Your purpose. He was willing to give up all so we might become joint-heirs with Him. He had us in mind on that cross. He willingly gave of His life so we might gain eternal life.

Raise up men of God who are passionate to serve You, as Jesus did, with their whole hearts. By faith each will teach their children Your ways as they go about their days. They won't beat their children, either verbally or literally, with man-made religious rules so they develop hearts of stone. These husbands/fathers will cultivate tender hearts for You in their homes and instill in each a hunger and ability to hear Your voice. They will lead primarily by being an imitator of Jesus Christ and walking in His love.

Being a godly leader in the home is impossible without Your grace and Your Holy Spirit working in each man's life. So many throw in the towel and flee when the road gets tough. Millions of women and children have been abandoned by their husbands/fathers. Where are these protectors, these champions?

Restore the hearts of these fallen husbands and fathers to their families. Strengthen feeble hearts. Transform angry tempers. Emblazon despondent souls with Your hope, compassion, and faith. Teach their mouths how to bless and not curse. How blessed is the man who can manage his household with dignity and grace for he will hear You say, "Well done, My good and faithful servant."

Phil. 2:5-8; 2 Cor. 8:9; Deut. 6:5-9; Ez. 11:19; Mal. 4:6;
Prov. 18:21; 1 Tim. 3:2-4; Matt. 25:23

19. Malnutrition

Because of drought, overgrazing, deforestation, soil depletion, greed, government policies, and warfare, both scarcities of food and vitamin/mineral deficiencies abound. Barrenness in nature does not reflect Your glory. Most of these tragedies have not been brought on by You, Most Gracious Father, but by mankind. Strengthen those who endeavor to fight these curses like You did with Elisha of old.

Empower the efforts of those who are working in impoverished communities to re-establish healthy environments so Your creation can flourish. Thwart the plans of those who are altering foods from Your unique design. You originally created our world in perfect harmony. Since You commanded mankind to rule over and subdue the earth, we can be confident that You will also grant blessing when we labor diligently to care for Your creation in a way that will bring glory to You.

Many thousands of families around the world witness malnutrition ravaging their loved ones. With rising food prices all over the world, the meager "dollar" millions have each day for food stretches less and less. You know their pain and their struggles, and You care. Jesus understood how important day-to-day nourishment was. Much of His life and several of His miracles pertained to food, especially daily bread. In Your mercy, give them their daily bread, *Jehovah-Jireh* (the LORD Will Provide).

Thousands of parents in their own wisdom reason they must sacrifice one daughter, selling her into slavery, to purchase food for the rest of their children. O, Bread of Life, they do not know You and Your ability and willingness to multiply and care for each and every one in the family! Show them Your providing power and increase their faith. Visit Your people, Heavenly Father. Especially provide miraculously for the little ones who are generally the most vulnerable.

Rom. 8:20-22; I Kings 2:19-22; Gen. 1:28-31;
Prov. 10:4; Matt. 6:11; Ps. 34:9-10

20. Modern Day Slavery & Pornography

We live in an age to fight for human freedom. To battle against the rulers, powers, and world forces of this darkness, we must put on the full armor You have provided for us. Remind us daily, as we stand firm against the prince of this world. Moral decadence of any kind is abhorrent to Your attributes of love, holiness, and purity. Oh, *Elohim* (the God of Power and Might), only You can break through the chains of modern-day slavery. Your Son, Jesus, broke the curse of death and sin; He has the power to shatter slave trade, sex trafficking, and pornography.

May women and children find Your grace in this viper's pit where they feel lost, abandoned, and forgotten. Supernaturally heal their broken bones and bruised bodies; restore their minds blown out by drugs to make them compliant. Draw them to Yourself with Your everlasting love. May they know Your Father-heart, which weeps at what has been/is being done to them. Even when they cannot yet escape the horrors surrounding them, be their refuge, their fortress, their hope, and their joy—impossibilities apart from You being the God of the Universe.

May Your Spirit bless the hands of those who are working to set the captives free, for it is Your work. Lighten their load; carry their burden for it is too great for them to bear. Bring more people and resources to stand, work, and pray alongside them. Multiply what they do supernaturally so more and more women and children caught in Satan's steel trap are set free. Enlighten and empower those who care for them afterwards in finding housing, food, employment, emotional counseling, protection, and restore them with their families.

Bring an end to the suffering of women and children.

Eph. 6:10-17; Gal. 3:13; Ps. 136:23; Ps. 46:1; Is. 61:1; Ps. 68:19; Gal. 6:2

21. Morality

King of Kings, confusion reigns in nations and cultures today in what constitutes right and wrong. People call the good evil and the evil good. How is a person to know?

Many believe money holds the answers to basic questions of life. Gold…so many want it, Lord. Wars are fought even today over the control of it. However, there is something more desirable than gold. It is perfect; it restores the soul; it makes the simple wise; it rejoices the heart and enlightens the eyes. An entire Psalm—176 verses!—expounds on the beauty and wonder of Your statutes. How we love Your Word! When we have lost our way, Your precepts bring us back. When we struggle with doing what is right, Your commandments show us the way. When we don't understand what is happening, Your testimonies are our counselors.

People have inflicted despicable evils on innocents because they thought they had license to do so. Anything can seem right in our own sinful hearts, but unless the foundation of righteousness and justice is in You, it is erroneous. Because of Your love and Your desire to bless Your children, You made morality clear for all. To those who do not want to acknowledge You and Your ways, bring them to repentance and heal their depraved minds.

The only standard that is always true is Your Word, the Bible. The hurting women and children of this world need to know Your absolutes. Chastise those who confuse these precious ones of what is right and wrong. If they don't have any portion of scripture or cannot read, through Your Spirit speak Your truths into their hearts. Remove the scales the enemy has placed on their eyes so they can know the Truth and be free!

Is. 5:20; Ps. 19:7-10; Ps. 119; Prov. 14:12; Ps. 89:14; Jn. 6:68-9; Jn. 8:32

22. Physical & Emotional Healing

Show in a miraculous way today Your power to bind up the broken-hearted. Their bodies, their lives, and their hope hang in the balance. Comfort those who mourn. Millions each day need Your healing touch on their broken, ripped, mutilated, and bruised bodies. Only You can exchange the ashes these women and children live in for a garland, one specifically and lovingly fashioned individually for each one.

Though difficult to see from a human perspective, there is nothing or no one who can separate them from Your love. However, sin has so obscured Your love; these precious ones have a tough time seeing it. Wherever there is an opening, beam Your love into their hearts. Provide a way for women and children to get out of the abusive situation in which they are trapped.

The world says these women and children will never be able to recover from the horrors inflicted upon them. But we stand today upon Your Word which declares that nothing is impossible or too hard for You. You can take mourning and exchange it for the oil of gladness. By the power of Your Spirit, You can carry those who faint and put on them a mantle of praise. You alone are their Hope. Thank You for Your Spirit who prays for them in moans too deep for words. Bring Spirit-filled believers into the lives of those who are hungering for release. Bless their prayer ministry of deliverance from the strongholds surrounding these women.

Part of healing comes with being able to share what has happened to them. To keep it hidden will only encourage more evil. Bringing it out into the light requires tremendous valor. Give women and children the courage to find their voice and tell their stories. Protect them as they do.

Is. 61:1-2; 2 Cor. 1:3; Rom. 8:38-39; Jer. 32:27; Rm. 8:26-28

23. The Poor

Jesus said that the poor would always be with us. However, You charged us, Your children, to not harden our hearts or to shut our hands from our poor brethren. *El-Olam* (the Everlasting God), You have blessed many around the world with more than what is needed. Open our eyes, ears, and hearts to Your Spirit. Perhaps there is more You would have us to do.

Some women are struggling now because they have not been faithful to return the tithe to You or have turned their face from the poor in the past. Where they are, right now in their poverty, encourage them to be obedient. Then open the floodgates and bless them with increase in whatever way You deem best.

Reveal where poor family choices and sins of the past have entrapped women and children so these sins can be brought to the cross to be broken and Your blessing restored. Bring to light where there has been dishonest gain. May these women and children follow Zaccheus's example to make restitution as You lead. Thank You for Jesus being our Advocate and forgiving sins regarding money. Convict the hearts of the lazy, the undisciplined, or those women and teens that hold to a feeling of entitlement. Bring them to repentance and provide a means for each to support themselves and their loved ones.

Under Your almighty wings, shelter and provide for those who are poor because of unforeseen, disastrous events beyond their control. Arouse believers around the world to come to their aid and reestablish each. Break the strength of those who have a love for money. Because of their greed, they have oppressed the poor rather than relieving their distress. In faith they will be caught in the schemes they have devised.

Deut. 15:7; Is. 40:28-31; Ez. 16:49; Mal. 3:8-10;
Prov. 22:9; Prov. 13:11; Lk. 19:8; I Jn. 2:1

24. Prison Reform

El-Shaddai (God Almighty), burden those in the penal system to understand the circumstances of the past that led female inmates to where they are today, especially if they are women of color or a different tribe or people group. Bless the work of those inside and outside the prisons whether it is evangelism, Bible studies, education, life skills, vocational training, or counseling. Protect female inmates from further abuse while in jail.

Vindicate those women and girls who have been wrongly accused and incarcerated. Convict the hearts of the women and girls who have strayed from You either intentionally or because they believed there to be no other option. Release these women from the ironclad chains of syndicate crime and drugs. Breathe hope into their spirits and souls.

The great majority of those arrested in prostitution, trafficking, or substance abuse end up back on the street and doing drugs with their "daddy", their pimp. Oh, Father! You are their true *Abba*, Daddy! Remove the scales from their eyes and the strongholds in their lives so these lovely ones can see You and Your provision for them. Open their hearts to the blessings and victories You have for them as new creatures in Christ. Proclaim Your freedom to these captives.

Show mercy to those under-sixteen girls who are arrested on the streets. May they not be placed in adult prisons and tried as adults. Raise up ministries that are able to compassionately and comprehensively rehabilitate these girls to get them off the street or substance abuse and into churches, homes, and schools where they can grow and develop into the godly women You desire them to be. You command us to compassionately remember in prayer and deed those who are in prison. May we not fail You.

Heb. 10:34; 2 Cor. 5:17; Ps. 69:33; Ps. 71:4-5; Is. 42:7;
Is. 61:1; Matt. 25:36

25. Religious Freedom & Persecution

Christian believers are being targeted for their faith all over the world today. Thank You, Father, that even now Jesus is making intercession for women and children who are facing persecution and lack religious freedom simply because of their gender or age. We will not be silent about this genocide. Honor killings, acid throwing, and bride burnings still claim young women. Only the power of the Gospel can change these harsh cultural practices.

In addition, place Your wall of protection around Christian churches and those Christian-owned businesses in areas that are notorious for vandalizing, burning, and bombing. Strengthen the leaders in the underground church. Shelter them in the shadow of Your Almighty Wings. You are their Hiding Place. They will shout of Your deliverance.

Hide individual believers in the blood of Jesus. Their faith will be fortified as they see You deliver them from the snares of evil men. Foil the plans of those who intend harm. You are their shield and their rampart. Be the defense of their life. Encourage those who are suffering for the sake of righteousness. Calm any fears. In Your mercy and grace, grant them the peace that rises above the difficulties looming over them.

Jehovah-Sabaoth (the LORD of Hosts), work peace and stability in the lives of those who have chosen to follow You in spite of great opposition, beatings, jailing, and/or even death. Should death in this present world come, comfort and provide for their loved ones left behind. May You use human tragedy to build Your Church which will stand victorious forevermore. Father, You are able to grieve with those whose loved ones have shed blood for their faith because Your very own Son purchased salvation with His blood for all who believe.

Heb. 7:25; Ps. 91:1-4; Ps. 32:7; Ps. 27:1; I Pet. 3:14; Phil. 4:6-7; Is. 6:1-3

26. Repentance & Holiness in the Church

You desire men and women who trust in You to build up the wall and stand in the gap. The gap before us is a chasm: slavery, oppression, robbery, rape, abortion, and injustice to the poor and needy — especially to women and children.

We cannot stand before a holy God. *Jehovah Maccaddeshem* (the LORD thy Sanctifier), You are the Lord who sanctifies us. Any who hide sin will not prosper for eternity. Daily remind us to come to the throne of grace to confess and forsake our transgressions and find compassion, forgiveness, and healing. May we have our hearts sprinkled clean from all evil so we can be holy as You are holy.

You desire us to be uncorrupted, blameless, and innocent so that we are Spirit-filled lights shining forth Your glory in the darkness around. To those who refuse, You are the Refiner's Fire to burn off all the chaff and impurities. How You hate duplicity, especially in Your Church! We must be people who talk and walk the fruit of the Spirit. Jesus had kinder words to flagrant sinners than He did to those who were religious hypocrites. Great calamity and ruin come to Your people who do not turn from all transgressions.

There have been many women and children who have been wounded or desecrated by individuals in the Church. Perhaps it has been unkind, mocking words or outright lies, perhaps deception or insensitivity, perhaps far worse. And because of our disregard of Your holiness in our lives, we have pushed some away from You. Bring these sins to light. Forgive us. Show us any restitution we can do, and give us the courage to follow through. Reprove and discipline us individually and corporately. We need revival! The time is now; Your kingdom is at hand.

Ez. 22:29-30; Ex. 31:13; Prov. 28:13; Heb. 10:22; I Pet. 1:16; Phil. 2:15; Mal. 3:2; Rev. 3:19

27. Sexual Purity — Before & Within Marriage

How Your heart aches when we have not followed the pattern so clearly laid out. Your plan is for marriage between one man and one woman to be a reflection of Jesus and Your Church. Everywhere we look today (TV, movies, music, books, advertisements, and magazines) sexual purity is being assaulted, O Holy One of Israel. When You gave Moses directions for the tabernacle, everything was to be pure and holy. Now our bodies are Your temple. We cannot do whatever we want and expect Your blessing. We were bought with the precious blood of Jesus for a purpose—to glorify You in our bodies.

You will not spare those who fall into sexual sins: pre-marital sex, prostitution, rape, homosexuality, adultery, incest, or bestiality. You hate it because sexual iniquity is so destructive: to the individual, to the family, to the church, to the culture, and to the nation.

We will stand. We will fight against the enemy who delights in impurity and unfaithfulness. We fight in the power of the Holy Spirit with our example of being pure ourselves, with our teaching our children the joys of purity, and in grace-filled, appropriate ministry opportunities. Soften our hearts and words, Lord, so that we will stand alongside and uphold a man, woman, or couple who have slipped. May we not judge but forgive, being careful to look to our own sin propensity. Give us the balance between upholding and proclaiming penitence and redemption, grace and law, and truth and mercy.

Increase the desire for purity in men and women, teens and children. As they grow in purity of heart, they will see You in greater dimensions. Work in Your people around the world to find ethnic solutions to practices like unrealistic bride prices and dowries that encourage impropriety and immorality.

Deut. 7:6; Eph. 5:22-33; I Cor. 6:15-20; I Cor. 7:23; Gal. 6:1; Matt. 5:8

28. Stolen Childhoods

Children around the world are missing, forced into the streets, or commandeered into war, slavery, or sex. They do not have a safe place to flourish and mature. So many millions have been drugged, beaten, and coerced to do things that would normally be abhorrent to them. Right now, these precious ones are confused, frightened, and hopeless. There is no one like You, O Lord, who can save them. Be their stronghold in times of trouble. Bring these children to Jesus so He might gather them into His arms and bless them.

Today be the God of all comfort in some way to each. Because of Your great love and tender mercy, shine upon these children in their darkness and shadow of death. Guide their feet into the way of peace. Set them free! Bring believers into their lives to help them sort out all the rejection, lies, and deceit forced upon them. Their sweet voices will sing praises to Your name. They will give You thanks among the nations for rescuing them from violent men and women.

Woe to those who cause little ones who believe in You to stumble! It is better for them to tie a heavy rock around their necks and throw themselves into the sea.

We grieve with those who do not know where their child/ren is/are. Is he/she alive? Hungry? Ill? In pain or danger? The questions never cease. Their child is never far from their thoughts and prayers. Dear Father, comfort these parents. Give them the peace that passes all understanding. Supernaturally return these children to their families. Bring Spirit-filled believers to support, listen, and counsel as all in the family work through the myriad of spiritual, financial, emotional, and relational issues. *Jehovah-Nissi* (the LORD our Banner), set up Your banner of love over these families.

Ps. 59:9; Mk. 10:13-16; Lk. 1:78-9; Ps. 18:48-9;
Matt. 18:6; Phil. 4:7; Song 2:4

29. Violence as a Culture & War Crimes

We appeal to You, *Jehovah-Shalom* (the LORD our Peace). So many women and children have been wronged, abused, tortured, and killed. Millions have been raped and maimed as weapons of war. We cannot know the full story of each one, but You do, and it grieves You. Mighty One, You will never forget. You will never abandon Your creation and Your children.

Increase Your angels to surround each of them. Keep them from the Path of the Destroyer. Hide them in the blood of Your Son. As they learn about You, they will call upon You, and You will be with them and rescue them. In faith, these precious ones will dwell in the shelter of the Most High. They will find refuge under Your wings.

We plead with You also to intervene and to repay. You hate those who love viciousness; You abhor men of violence. Vengeance is Yours, O *Jehovah-Gmolah* (the God of Recompense). Expose what has been done and continues to be done in areas where crimes against women and children are used to destabilize, terrorize, and subdue tribal, ethnic, or political conflicts. Many times the police and military are the perpetrators or accomplices. Replace them with Your servants who will uphold their God-given roles.

Aid those who endeavor to bring to justice the wrongs and evil done in war-torn areas. You see their oppression. Come and judge their case. Eventually Your enemies will stumble and perish before You. We draw near to the throne of God so these, Your children, may receive mercy and find grace to help in time of need. You have heard our voices. Do not hide Your ear from our prayers for relief. Blessed be Your name, God of Israel, who alone works wonders.

Is. 49:15; Ps. 91:11, 15; Jer. 51:6; Deut. 32:35; Lam. 3:56, 59;
Heb. 4:16; Ps. 72:18

30. Widows & Orphans

We want to be part of fulfilling the law of Christ by bearing the burdens of the widows and orphans around us. Keep us faithful in doing good. However, there are millions more in the world today who do not have the support of those around them. They need Your gentle, protective hand upon them, *Jehovah-Shammah* (the LORD is There). They will know deep in their souls how much You love them. The cry of their heart to You is, "*Abba*, Daddy." Increasingly the women and children will know that they can trust You.

Open the mouths of those who judge for the rights of the unfortunate. They will defend the afflicted and needy. They will speak up and dispense true justice so that no one can oppress the widow or the orphan, the stranger or the poor.

Raise up more men and women to look after the needs of widows and children. Strengthen the vulnerable ones physically, for often their health suffers. Many ministries are currently working tirelessly all over the world to care for Your loved ones. Give them creative ideas to channel widows into skills and vocations where they can learn to support themselves and their children. In faith You will use them in remarkable ways to further the Gospel.

Give these widows a passion for visiting the sick and bereaved, helping in their communities, and fasting and praying. They will especially reach out to other widows and orphans. You will use them to comfort and encourage others because they themselves have learned to come to You for their every need. Furthermore, their personal identity is found only in You, not in their past husband and the loss of status which often comes upon them in many parts of the world.

Gal. 6:2, 9; Jer. 49:11; Deut. 10:18; Zech. 7:9-10; Prov. 31:8-9;
Acts 6:1-3; Acts 9:36-9; 1 Tim. 5:9-10

Notes for Further Prayer

1. Access to Scripture

- ❋ There are around 6,600 languages in the world.[1]
- ❋ Only 1,231 languages have the New Testament.[1]
- ❋ United Bible Societies are currently translating God's Word into 500 languages.[1]
- ❋ Less than 93% of these languages have a complete Bible.[2]
- ❋ There are still 1,900+ languages that have no Scripture whatsoever.[2]
- ❋ About 180 million people speak languages where Bible translation has not yet begun.[2]
- ❋ The three areas of greatest need for the Scripture: Central Africa/Nigeria, Mainland/Southeast Asia, and Indonesia/Pacific Islands.[2]
- ❋ Every year there are around 78.5 million Bibles distributed.[3]

[1] "Translation." *Biblesociety.org.nz.* 2013. Web. 03 Mar. 2014.
[2] "Translation Statistics." *Wycliffe.org.* 2014. Web. 03 Mar. 2014.
[3] Fairchild, Mary. "Christianity Today – General Statistics and Facts of Christianity." *Christianity.about.com.* 2012. Web. 03 Mar. 2014.

2. Blessing of the Land & Farming

- ❋ Many people in the world do not have enough land to grow the food needed to support their family.[1]
- ❋ Nearly one in eight of the 7.1 billion in the world today suffer from chronic undernourishment.[1]

[1] "2013 World Hunger and Poverty Facts and Statistics." *Worldhunger.org.* 2013. Web. 03 Mar. 2014.

3. Businesses by Women

❈ The question is not who is better, men or women, at any given task. The challenge is to encourage each member of society to reach their God-given potential, using the gifts and abilities He has given them to fulfill His purposes for their lives (personal view).

❈ "Empowering female business owners can improve economies around the world."[1]

❈ Most barriers facing women in small and medium-sized business concern poor access to finances and resources.[1]

❈ The surest method to build thriving and secure societies is to encourage women to succeed economically and in political and civil leadership.[1]

❈ "One study estimated that lowering barriers to women's economic participation in emerging economies could raise per capita incomes as much as 14 percent. Larger incomes mean more money to feed families, send children to school, and support local merchants and producers, igniting a virtuous circle of economic growth."[2]

❈ Worldwide two out of five workers are women but 50% are in vulnerable positions and beyond the reach of labor laws.[3]

[1] Milligan, Susan. "U.S. Officials Support Businesswomen Worldwide." *iipdigital.usembassy.gov*. 28 Oct. 2011. Web. 06 Dec. 2011.

[2] Clinton, Hillary Rodham. "16 Days of Activism Against Gender Violence." *yaounde.usembassy.gov*. 08 Dec. 2011. Web. 13 Dec. 2011.

[3] Mlambo-Ngcuka, Phumzile. "The Knowledge Gateway." Unwomen.org. 23 Sept. 2013. Web. 03 Mar. 2014.

4. Church Leaders Become Shepherds

❈ 26% said they had personal devotions and were satisfied with their own spiritual growth.[1]

❈ One out of three pastors felt completely burned out after five years of ministry.[1]

❈ One out of three felt it was "clearly hazardous for their families."[1]

- ✶ Less than 30% of pastors felt they had a friend. Hardly any had a close friend.[1]
- ✶ In general, clergy have a higher rate of obesity, hypertension, and depression than most Americans.[2]
- ✶ 70% of pastors fight depression.[3]
- ✶ *If you have made it this far, stop and spend some time praying for your pastor.*

[1] Krejcir, Dr. Richard. "Statistics on Pastors." *Intothyword.org.* 2007. Web. 19 Mar. 2012.
[2] Croucher, Rowland and others. "Pastor Burnout Statistics." *Jmm. aaa.net.au.* 20 June 2011. Web. 19 Mar. 2012.
[3] Murphy, Richard. "Statistics About Pastors." *maranathalife.com.* 2002. Web. 19 Mar. 2012.

5. Church/Missionary Access

- ✶ In research up to 2006, 50% of Americans had no church home.[1]
- ✶ In the U.S. over 1000 new churches start each year; however, 4000 churches shut down.[1]
- ✶ In 1900 there were 27 churches for every 10,000 individuals in America. In 2000 there are only 11 churches for the same number of people.[1]
- ✶ In 2002 only 18% attended any kind of church in the U.S.[1]
- ✶ Only China and India surpass the U.S. in the number of non-professing Christians.[1]
- ✶ 23% of the world's population is considered to be Christian: Roman Catholic (1+ billion), Protestant (800 million), Eastern Orthodox (260 million) [2]
- ✶ 95% of full-time Christian workers work within the Christian world.[2]
- ✶ "If the ratio of Christian workers to total population that exists in North Africa were applied to the U.S. and Canada, those two countries would have about 120 full-time Christian workers living in them. Also, there would be only seven small churches in the entirety of those two countries."[3]
- ✶ By 2020, 64.7% of all Christians are expected to live in the global South.[4]

- ✳ In W. Asia and N. Africa only 10-11% of the population is thought to personally know a Christian.[4]
- ✳ More people in W. Africa (24%) than in any region in Europe know a Christian.[4]

[1] Krejcir, Dr. Richard J. "Statistics and Reasons for Church Decline." *Churchleadership.org.* 2007. Web. 19 Mar. 2012.

[2] Fairchild, Mary. "Christianity Today – General Statistics and Facts of Christianity." *Christianity.about.com.* 2012. Web. 21 Mar. 2012.

[3] Culbertson, Howard. "Harvest is great; workers are few." *Home. snu.edu.* 31 Aug. 2009. Web. 21 Mar. 2012.

[4] "Christianity in its Global Context, 1970-2020." *Gordonconwell. com.* June 2013. Web. 03 Mar. 2014.

6. Corruption, Lying, & Stealing

- ✳ Corruption Perceptions Index (CPI) measures "the abuse of public power and focus on: bribery of public officials, kickback in public procurement, embezzlement of public funds, and on questions that probe the strength and effectiveness of anti-corruption efforts in the public sector."[1]
- ✳ Of 177 countries, two-fifths have less than 50/100 points in the CPI 2013.[1]
- ✳ It is difficult to measure absolute corruption. In general, perceived corruption is based on illegal activities that appear in scandals, investigations, or prosecutions.[1]
- ✳ Africa, the Middle East, and Russia have the highest concentrations of perceived corruption.[1]
- ✳ Only 37% of those surveyed worldwide believe that a high ranking government official would be prosecuted and punished for stealing government money.[2]
- ✳ "A culture of impunity undermines respect for fundamental rights, breeds corruption, and leads to a vicious cycle of law-breaking…"[2]

[1] "In Detail." *Cpi.transparency.org.* 2013. Web. 03 Mar. 2014.

[2] "The WJR Rule of Law Index 2012-2013". *Worldjusticeproject.org.* 2012. Web.pdf. 04 Mar. 2014.

7. Discipleship & Spiritual Growth

※ "Go therefore and make disciples of all the nations, baptizing them in the name of the Father and the Son and the Holy Spirit, teaching them to observe all that I commanded you; and lo, I am with you always, even to the end of the age" (Matt. 28:19-20).

※ 81% of pastors (Reformed and Evangelical) interviewed said their church had no regular discipleship or mentoring program.[1]

[1] Krejcir, Dr. Richard. "Statistics on Pastors." *Intothyword.org.* 2007. Web. 19 Mar. 2012.

8. Education of Girls & Freedom

※ Of those who are illiterate, 66% are women (Miller 32).

※ Families in xx sell their virgin daughters to the highest bidder for a couple of weeks, after which the girl returns to home and school (Batstone, loc 904-7).

※ "For every one thousand girls who get one additional year of education, two fewer women will die in childbirth." (Kristof and WuDunn114).

※ Around the world, one in ten girls are married before 15 with India significantly hightest.[1]

※ Worldwide in 2011, 57 million primary-aged children were not attending school.[2]

※ More than one-fifth of sub-Saharan children never attended school or left before finishing primary school.[2]

※ "Rural children are twice as likely to be out of school as urban children.... Children from the poorest quintile are nearly four times as likely to be out of school..."[2]

※ Only 6% of university age adults were enrolled in 2008 in sub-Sahara Africa.[3]

※ "Only 62 out of 168 countries are expected to reach gender parity in secondary education by 2015."[4]

[1] "Statistics on Child Marriage." *Filipspagnoli.wordpress. com.* n.d. Web. Statistics on Abandoned Children." *Internationalstreetkids.com.* 2014. Web. 03 Mar. 2014.

[2] "Progress towards Universal Primary Education Too Slow." *uis. unesco.org.* June 2013, No. 25. Web.pdf. 03 Mar. 2014.

[3] "Trends in Tertiary Education: Sub-Saharan Africa." *uis.unesco. org.* December 2010. Web.pdf. 13 Dec. 2011.

[4] Bachelet, Michelle. "Addressing Inequalities in the post-2015 Development Agenda." *unwomen.org.* 19 Feb. 2013. Web. 4 Mar. 2014.

10. Equality of Women & Value as Individuals

- ※ More than 100,000,000 women are not here because of neglect (Miller 20).
- ※ Eighty percent of those trafficked out of poor countries are women (Batstone, Loc 156-57).
- ※ In southeast Asia, a brothel owner can purchase a woman or child for $50 (Batstone, Loc 361-64).
- ※ Buddhism sees women as second-class. It is assumed to be born a woman means a sinful life in a prior life (Batstone, Loc. 811-15).
- ※ In Uganda, the LRA teaches their soldiers that women are "creatures that exist to serve their pleasures" (Batstone, Loc 2005-7).
- ※ In many countries of the world only men can transfer their nationality to their children. This can affect a woman and her children in obtaining legal and basic services and rights.[1]
- ※ In sub-Saharan Africa 50%+ did not have a voice on matters concerning "their own health care, household purchases, or visits to family."[1]
- ※ "Human trafficking is a global phenomenon that is fueled by poverty and gender discrimination."[2]
- ※ Women (and men and children) are trafficked for organ harvesting.[2]

[1] "Factsheet: Sub-Saharan Africa." Progress of the World's Women 2011-2012. progress.unwomen.org. Web. 03 Dec. 2011.

[2] "55 Little Known Facts About Human Trafficking." Facts. randomhistory.com. 02 Jan. 2011. Web. 19 Nov. 2011.

13. The Family

- ❀ In many Southeast Asian countries over half the population is under 15 years old (Batstone, Loc 357-58).
- ❀ Many sex slaves are obtained through "lover boys" who approach young, vulnerable girls and make promises of love and a better life (Kara, Loc 397).
- ❀ "15.5 million children in the United States live in families in which partner violence occurred at least once in the past year."[1]
- ❀ Father-absent homes raises the risk of delinquency, teen pregnancy, and not finishing high school.[2]
- ❀ One out of three children in the U.S. live in a home without their biological father.[2]
- ❀ "Children in father-absent homes are almost four times more likely to be poor."[2]
- ❀ "Infant mortality rates are 1.8 times higher for infants of unmarried mothers than for married mothers."[2]

[1] "Get the Facts: The Facts on Domestic, Dating and Sexual Violence." *futureswithoutviolence.org.* n.d. Web. 25 Nov. 2011.

[2] "Statistics on the Father Absence Crisis in America." *Fatherhood. org.* n.d. Web. 04 Mar. 2014.

15. Health Care & AIDS

- ❀ Worldwide 600,000 (estimated) women die in childbirth yearly (Miller 32).
- ❀ Every three minutes a baby dies in India from diarrhea (Skinner 291).
- ❀ Debt bondage (slavery conditions due to debt) occurs most frequently in a family health crisis (Skinner 291).
- ❀ "Sex trafficking plays a major role in the spread of HIV."[1]
- ❀ In 2012 an estimated 35.2 million people were living with HIV and 1.6 million died from AIDS.[2]
- ❀ A third of the women in developing countries marry by 18. Death in pregnancy and childbirth is the number one cause of death for girls 15-19.[3]

[1] "55 Little Known Facts About Human Trafficking." *Facts. randomhistory.com.* 02 Jan. 2011. Web. 29 Nov. 2011.

[2] "Global Report 2013." *Unaids.org.* 2013. Web.pdf. 04 Mar. 2014.

[3] "Factsheet: Global." *Progress of World's Women 2011-2012. Progress.unwomen.org.* n.d. Web. 17 Nov. 2011.

16. Infant Mortality & Abortion

✱ 46,000,000 abortions occur yearly worldwide — the majority of them are girls (Miller 27,30).

✱ Every year 1,000,000 baby girls are left to die in China — simply because they aren't boys (Miller 30).

✱ Miscarriages, stillbirths, preterm delivery and low birth weight babies are higher where there has been intimate partner violence.[1]

[1] "Violence against Women: Intimate Partner and Sexual Violence Against Women." "Fact sheet #239." *who.int.* Oct. 2013. Web. 04 Mar. 2014.

17. Justice

✱ International Justice Mission does not usually work with the lowest level of police officers since they are more likely to be tied up with the perpetrators (Batstone 88).

✱ The U.S. spends $4.2 billion each year to help in justice reform, but only 5% specifically targets women and girls (half of the population!). Domestic violence is not considered a crime in countries housing 603 million women.[1]

✱ Obtaining justice is often too costly for the majority of women in the world. Corruption and bribery are high. The location of the courts is hard to reach for the poor.[2] There is a high drop-out rate for women seeking justice on gender-based violence.[1]

✱ Marital rape has not been criminalized in countries for 2.6 billion women.[1]

✱ Even though 117 countries have equal pay laws, women are still paid 10-30% less in some countries in the world. When women make up 30% of a nation's parliament, greater progress is made in women's rights (voting, workplace, family, and property and inheritance). Lack of sexual harassment laws affects 311 million working age women. Progress has been made legally for ownership and inheritance rights for women.[1]

❁ Countries with a well-function criminal justice system generally have less crime. "Crime rates in Latin America are among the highest in the world."[2]

❁ Sub-Saharan Africa and South Asia as regions lag behind other regions around the world in most dimensions of the rule of law.[2]

[1] "Justice Still out of Reach for Millions of Women, UN Women Says." unwomen.org. 06 July 2011. Web. 17 Nov. 2011.
[2] "The WJR Rule of Law Index 2012-2013". Worldjusticeproject.org. 2012. Web.pdf. 04 Mar. 2014.

19. Malnutrition

❁ There are two types of malnutrition: protein-energy (lacking enough calories and protein for bone and muscle growth as well as energy for work) and micronutrient deficiency (not usually included).[1]

❁ "Children who are poorly nourished suffer up to 160 days of illness each year. Poor nutrition plays a role in at least half of the 10.9 million child deaths each year—five million deaths."[1]

❁ Poor nutrition causes neonatal deaths, mental and learning disabilities, poor health, blindness, and premature death.[1]

[1] "2013 World Hunger and Poverty Facts and Statistics." Worldhunger.org. 2013. Web. 03 Mar. 2014.

20. Modern Day Slavery & Pornography

❁ The average sex slave is forced to have sex up to 20 times a day (Chestnut, loc 2685).

- More slaves exist today than in 400 years of the transatlantic slave trade (Batstone 6).
- India, Bangladesh, Nepal, and Pakistan contain at least 15 million bonded slaves (Batstone 11).
- Programs that merely free sex slaves but do not help them with training a job are usually not successful (Batstone 35).
- In Cambodia almost 35% of Vietnamese families sell a daughter into the sex trade (Batstone 56).
- Businesses use paid sex as benefit of commercial deals (Batstone 62).
- Some firms will lose customers to other firms if clients are not offered paid sex (Batstone 62).
- Because of China's population control practices, 111 million men cannot obtain a Chinese wife. Slave traders are supplying this need through trafficking from other countries (Miller 25).
- Dubai is "the fastest-growing destination for sex traffickers (Skinner 174).
- The International Labor Office estimates that the slave trade brings in $32 billion yearly (Batstone 4).
- Porn studios produce 11,000 films a year in the U.S. and bring in over $10 billion (Miller 23).
- "Trafficking ranks second, after drug smuggling and tying with arms dealing, in organized crime activities."[1]
- "There are an estimated 27 million adults and 13 million children around the world who are victims of human trafficking."[2]
- "The FBI estimates that over 100,000 children and young women are trafficked in American today. They range in age from 9 to 19, with the average being age 11."[2]
- "Eighty percent of those sold into sexual slavery are under 24, and some are a young as six years old."[2]
- "Approximately 75-80% of human trafficking is for sex." "Approximately 30,000 victims of sex trafficking die each year."[2]
- Conditioning victims include "starvation, rape, gang rape, physical abuse, beating, confinement, threats of violence toward the victim and victim's family, forced drug use, and shame."[2]

- ✳ Web sites are available for those who are interested in sex tourism.
- ✳ Countries on Tier 3 of Trafficking In Persons 2012 report: Algeria, Central African Republic, DR Congo, Cuba, Equatorial Guinea, Eritrea, Iran, N. Korea, Kuwait, Libya, Madagascar, Papua New Guinea, Saudi Arabia, Sudan, Syria, Yemen, and Zimbabwe (up four countries from 2010) [3]

[1] "A Serious Problem — Around the Globe and in the USA." *Castla. org. n.d.* Web. 22 Nov. 2011.
[2] "55 Little Known Facts About Human Trafficking." *Facts. randomhistory.com.* 02 Jan. 2011. Web. 29 Nov. 2011.
[3] "Trafficking in Persons Report 2012." *State.gov.* June 2012. Web. pdf. 4 Mar. 2014.

21. Morality
- ✳ *"For the scepter of wickedness shall not rest upon the land of the righteous, So that the righteous will not put forth their hands to do wrong"* (Psalm 125:3).
- ✳ The presence of UN peacekeepers in the Balkans in the 1990s meant great profits for traffickers (Skinner 145).
- ✳ In southern Sudan, the price for a gun was more than a child slave in the 1990s (Skinner 82).

22. Physical & Emotional Healing
- ✳ "Domestic violence is the number one health risk for American women between the ages of fifteen and forty-five" (Miller 21).
- ✳ Every day just fewer than 6,000 girls are genitally mutilated [usually encouraged and performed by the women in the society] (Miller 28).
- ✳ Infibulation can cause many short term and long term risks including shock, infections, infertility, labor problems and even AIDS (Abusharaf 4).
- ✳ In the U.S. "women experience two million injuries from

intimate partner violence each year."[1]
- ❋ Almost 25% of U.S. women have experienced domestic violence.[1]
- ❋ "One in three adolescent girls in the United States is a victim of physical, emotional or verbal abuse from a dating partner."[1]
- ❋ Internationally 35% of women have experienced some kind of sexual violence in their lifetime.[2]
- ❋ "Sexual violence, particularly during childhood, can lead to increased smoking, drug and alcohol misuse, and risky sexual behaviors in later life."[2]
- ❋ Sexual violence "can lead to depression, post-traumatic stress disorder, sleep difficulties, eating disorders, emotional distress and suicide attempts."[2]
- ❋ "97% of married women in Egypt aged 15 to 49 have undergone female genital mutilation."[3]
- ❋ Statistics on violence against women must be interpreted with caution, as many women do not report it due to "discrimination, stigma, or even the threat of being killed."[3]
- ❋ The majority of women in the following countries never told anyone of their physical abuse/rape or sought help: Egypt 47%, Chile 97%, Ireland 80%, Australia 18%, Russian Federation 40%, UK 87%, and Bangladesh 68%...USA 84%.[3]

[1] "Get the Facts: The Facts on Domestic, Dating and Sexual Violence." *futureswithoutviolence.org*. 2014. Web. 05 Mar. 2014.
[2] "Violence against Women." "Fact sheet #239." *who.int*. October 2013. Web. 05 Mar. 2014.
[3] "Making Violence against Women Count: Facts and Figures — a Summary." *Amnesty International. religiousconsultation.org*. 03 May 2004. Web. 03 Dec. 2011.

23. The Poor
- ❋ Poverty is a major component in modern slavery (Skinner 52).
- ❋ In extreme poverty, slavery becomes a "tempting financial solution" (Batstone 23).

* Selling a daughter in "moments of financial need does not raise an eyebrow in most sectors of Southeast Asia" (Batstone 55).
* In the state of Bihar, India poor families often face the choice of watching their children starve, selling them as a slave, or giving them to radical Muslims (Skinner 235).
* Of all the children in the world, one out of every two lives in poverty (Shah 4).
* The gap between the rich and the poor is getting wider and more established (Shah 8).
* Those who are in debt bondage far surpass any other type of slavery (Skinner 229).
* More and more women are selling their newborns on the black market, some for as little as a few hundred dollars.[1]
* There were 890 million people chronically undernourished in the world as of 2012 (1 in 8).[2]
* The World Bank estimated in 2005 that 1.3 billion people lived on $1.25 or less a day.[2]
* The number of people living in extreme poverty in Sub-Saharan Africa has increased.[2]
* Poor nutrition contributes in the 5 million deaths of children each year.[2]

[1] "55 Little Known Facts About Human Trafficking." *facts. randomhistory.com.* 02 Jan. 2011. Web. 29 Nov. 2011.
[2] "2013 World Hunger and Poverty Facts and Statistics." *Worldhunger.org.* 2013. Web. 05 Mar. 2014.

25. Religious Freedom & Persecution
* "An average of 159,960 Christians worldwide are martyred for their faith per year.[1]
* "There are more than 65 countries where Christians are persecuted."[2]

[1] Fairchild, Mary. "Christianity Today – General Statistics and Facts of Christianity." *Christianity.about.com.* 2012. Web. 21 Mar. 2012.
[2] "FAQ." *worldwatchlist.us.* 2014. Web. 03 Mar. 2014.

26. Repentance & Holiness in the Church

※ In a poll 91% of people polled said that conflict and gossip was the main reason they had left going to church.[1]

※ The second reason was "the hypocrisy and judgmental attitude and actions of people."[1]

※ The fourth reason was "the unwillingness to deal with sin."[1]

※ More than 79% of adults in the U.S. identify themselves as Christian.[2]

[1] Krejcir, Dr. Richard J. "Why Churches Fail: Part I." *churchleadership.org*. 2007. Web. 19 Mar. 2012.

[2] Fairchild, Mary. "Christianity Today – General Statistics and Facts of Christianity." *Christianity.about.com*. 2014. Web. 05 Mar. 2014.

27. Sexual Purity

※ "The largest group of viewers of Internet porn is children between ages 12 and 17."[1]

※ In August 2005 the total number of people visiting porn was 71.9 million.[1]

※ Porn was a "current struggle" with 37% of pastors surveyed.[1]

※ Of high school students surveyed, 33.7% had had sexual intercourse in the past 3 months.[2]

※ "Nearly half of the 19 million new STDs each year are among young people aged 15–24 years."[2]

[1] "Pornography Statistics." *porntopurity.com*. n.d. Web. 05 Mar. 2015.

[2] "Sexual Risk Behavior." *cdc.gov*. 26 Aug. 2013. Web. 05 Mar. 2015.

28. Stolen Childhoods

※ There are over 400 million street children in the world today.[1]

※ Child pornography is estimated to earn $20 billion annually.[1]
※ Nearly 10 million children work as prostitutes.[1]
※ "The Taliban buys children as young as seven years old to act as suicide bombers."[2]

[1] Statistics on Abandoned Children." *Internationalstreetkids.com.* 2014. Web. 03 Mar. 2014.
[2] "55 Little Known Facts About Human Trafficking." *Facts. randomhistory.com.* 02 Jan. 2011. Web. 29 Nov. 2011.

29. Violence as a Culture & War Crimes
※ Forced sterilization occurs in many poverty-stricken countries (Miller 26).
※ Honor killing occurs for about 5,000 women/girls every year (Miller 30).
※ The Lord's Resistance Army (LRA) have enslaved as many as forty thousand children, which is up to 80% of their ranks (Batstone 111-12).
※ The LRA usually enters rural villages at night to abduct children (Batstone 121).
※ About 30 thousand children walk each night to a safe shelter near a national army garrison (Batstone 121).
※ A commander can have four to five sex slaves at his disposal in the LRA (Batstone 130).
※ From 1995 to 2005 over 2 million children were killed as a tactic of war. "Six million more children have been disabled or seriously injured in wars over the last decade, and one million have been orphaned" (Singer 5).
※ Children as young as five to seven have been found armed for combat (Singer 6, 15, 19, 20).
※ Child soldiers have been found in 47 countries (Singer 15-26).
※ Girls under 18 are increasingly present in the armed forces (Singer 31-32).
※ Between 1/5 to 1/7 women worldwide will be raped sometime in their life.[1]
※ "Rape is used as a means of psychological warfare to terrorize the population, make people submissive."[2]

- ※ "Women in eastern DRC remain one of the most vulnerable population groups in the world."[2]
- ※ One in four men in South Africa admit to have performed a sexual assault.[3]
- ※ "UNICEF estimates that 300,000 children younger than 18 are currently trafficked to serve in armed conflicts worldwide."[4]

[1] "Rape and Sexual Assault". *Whitehouse.gov.* Jan. 2014. Web. 05 Mar. 2014.
[2] Palitza, Kristin. "DR Congo: No End to Mass Rapes: 'It's a Miserable Life'." *ipsnews.net.* 17 Oct. 2011. Web. 25 Nov. 2011.
[3] Rebombo, Dumisani. "South African rapist: 'Forgive me'." *news.bbc.co.uk.* 25 Jun. 2009. Web. 11 Nov. 2011.
[4] "55 Little Known Facts About Human Trafficking." *facts.randomhistory.com.* 02 Jan. 2011. Web. 29 Nov. 2011.

30. Widows & Orphans

- ※ Every two seconds, a child becomes an orphan.[1]
- ※ "In some parts of eastern DRC, around 50% of women are widows."[2]
- ※ In many countries widows are denied basic rights, suffer physical/verbal abuse, shame, poverty, and sometimes death.[2]

[1] "Statistics on Abandoned Children." *Internationalstreetkids.com.* 2014. Web. 03 Mar. 2014.
[2] "International Widows' Day: Background." *Un.org.* 23 Jun. 2011. Web. 05 Mar. 2014.

 *Books cited*

Abusharaf, Rogaia Mustafa. *Female Circumcision*. Philadelphia: Univ. of Penn. Press. 2006.

Bales, Kevin. *The Slave Next Door: Human Trafficking and Slavery in America*. Univ. of Calif. Press. 2009. Kindle edition.

Batstone, David. *Not for Sale*. HarperCollins. 2008. Kindle edition.

Chestnut, Pamala. *More Than Rice: A Journey through the Underworld of Human Trafficking*. Yorkshire. 2010. Kindle edition.

Fikkert, Brian, Steve Corbett, and John Perkins. *When Helping Hurts: How to Alleviate Poverty Without Hurting the Poor*. Moody Pub. 2009. Kindle edition.

Haugen, Gary. *Good News About Injustice*. IVP Books. 2009. Kindle edition.

Kara, Siddharth. *Sex Trafficking: Inside the Business of Modern Slavery*. Columbia University Press. 2009. Kindle edition.

Keller, Timothy. *Generous Justice: How God's Grace Makes Us Just*. Dutton Adult. 2010. Kindle edition.

Kristof, Nicholas and Sheryl WuDunn. *Half the Sky*. Vintage. 2009. Kindle edition.

Miller, Darrow L. with Stan Guthrie. *Nurturing the Nations*. Colorado Springs: Paternoster. 2007.

Shannon, Lisa. *A Thousand Sisters: My Journey into the Worst Place on Earth to Be a Woman*. Seal Press. 2010. Kindle edition.

Singer, P.W. *Children at War*. New York: Pantheon Books. 2005.

Skinner, E. Benjamin. *A Crime So Monstrous*. New York: Free Press. 2008.

Stearns, Jason K. *Dancing in the Glory of Monsters*. New York: PublicAffairs. 2011.

E-book locations are based on Kindle Model D00901.

Personal Notes or Months Completed (always grace)

_____ _____ _____ _____ _____ _____ _____

_____ _____ _____ _____ _____ _____ _____

_____ _____ _____ _____ _____ _____ _____

_____ _____ _____ _____ _____ _____ _____

_____ _____ _____ _____ _____ _____ _____

_____ _____ _____ _____ _____ _____ _____

_____ _____ _____ _____ _____ _____ _____

_____ _____ _____ _____ _____ _____ _____

_____ _____ _____ _____ _____ _____ _____

_____ _____ _____ _____ _____ _____ _____

_____ _____ _____ _____ _____ _____ _____

_____ _____ _____ _____ _____ _____ _____

_____ _____ _____ _____ _____ _____ _____

_____ _____ _____ _____ _____ _____ _____

Acknowledgements:

※ To my husband, Dan, who supported and encouraged me for almost three years — every step of the way
※ To Darlene Ewell and Morning Star Church [Red Feathers, Colorado] for your generous gifts
※ To Eaton Evangelical Free Church [Colorado], Doris Meeker, and Celeste Laufert for your encouragement and accounting help
※ To Tom Barnes for your helpful biblical suggestions
※ To Jocelyn Frey for showing me the power of text & photos
※ To Ron & Roz Wismer who believed in what I was doing from the beginning
※ To Jo Thompson who reminded me that the women of Congo are not "broken" but resilient and that their beauty endures
※ To Susan McGregor, Marilyn Gorenflo, Allie Bramon, Terra Birkemo, and Dawn Wills for your excellent advice
※ To the Pick-a-WooWoo Publishing staff for your professionalism and graciousness
※ To my seven cherubs who never doubted that their mama could write a book

Author

Karen graduated from the University of Northern Colorado with a degree in elementary education. She taught first grade and then joined staff with Cru for seven years. In 1986 Karen followed her heart and God's call to Zaire (DR Congo) as the fiancée of Daniel Carlson, a pilot/mechanic with Mission Aviation Fellowship. God blessed them with eight children. Even through evacuations, pillages, and a devastating fire, Karen's love for the Congolese continues. Currently in Lubumbashi, DR Congo, she wrote these prayers as her personal response to the horrors inflicted upon the women and children of DR Congo.

Photographer

Anastasia (Dan and Karen's oldest child) spent five months in Nepal for her Biblical studies internship with Moody Bible Institute-Spokane, Washington. All but the rose photo was taken during that time. She is currently serving a twenty-three month term with ReachGlobal in France where she is studying French, leading the music team, and assisting with the university student ministry of the International Christian Community of Lyon.